T0112042

THE LITTLE RED BOOK OF

GOLF WISDOM

THE LITTLE RED BOOK OF
GOLF WISDOM

Edited by Niels Aaboe

Skyhorse Publishing

Copyright © 2013 by Niels Aaboe
First paperback edition, 2022

All Rights Reserved. No part of this book may be reproduced in any manner without the express written consent of the publisher, except in the case of brief excerpts in critical reviews or articles. All inquiries should be addressed to Skyhorse Publishing, 307 West 36th Street, 11th Floor, New York, NY 10018.

Skyhorse Publishing books may be purchased in bulk at special discounts for sales promotion, corporate gifts, fund-raising, or educational purposes. Special editions can also be created to specifications. For details, contact the Special Sales Department, Skyhorse Publishing, 307 West 36th Street, 11th Floor, New York, NY 10018 or info@skyhorsepublishing.com.

Skyhorse® and Skyhorse Publishing® are registered trademarks of Skyhorse Publishing, Inc. ®, a Delaware corporation.

www.skyhorsepublishing.com

10 9 8 7 6 5 4 3 2 1

Library of Congress Cataloging-in-Publication Data is available on file.

ISBN: 978-1-5107-6783-6
Ebook ISBN: 978-1-62636-263-5

Printed in China

Contents

Introduction

Golf's origins are murky. No one knows for sure whether the first golfer teed off on the windswept headlands of Scotland, the frozen rivers and canals of Holland, or the rugged terrain of ancient China.

But the following piece of golfing history is certain: the first Scottish reference to the game appears in a proclamation issued by King James II in 1457. Alarmed by the threat of an English invasion, James outlawed the playing of golf (along with "futebaw") because it was interfering with his subjects' archery practice. James died three years later, but the ban remained in effect for sixty long years—which suggests that James's royal successors also saw golf as a needless distraction from more important matters.

More than five hundred years later, it is a sentiment with which many non-golfers would doubtless agree. What's the point of spending hours hitting a little white ball and then walking miles to find it? What pleasure is derived from having to hack out of underbrush and sand, sometimes in horrid weather, often rising at the crack of dawn in order to do it? And, since golf is an extremely difficult game to play well, why spend an inordinate amount of time (and money) doing something when the rewards are so meager?

These are all good questions. Yet the bewilderment of the non-golfer is more than matched by the passion of people who play the game. Golf is one of the most popular sports in the world, played by 60 million people in 120 countries, according to the International Golf Federation. It's the reason why officials in sun-scorched places like Arizona and Dubai import countless gallons of precious water—and then use them to build and maintain golf courses. It leads otherwise sensible people to haul heavy golf clubs through airports, onto buses, and along city streets as they try to hail cabs. But why?

This book attempts to answer the question by providing a compilation of interesting, wise, and often hilarious quotes about golf. As I researched the collection, I was struck by how people from very different walks of life have weighed in on the sport A.A. Milne called "the best game in the world at which to be bad." No one will be surprised to see Bob Hope quoted in these pages, or Mark Twain, or Gerald Ford, or Tiger Woods. But I'd wager that a quote from Ulysses S. Grant will raise a few eyebrows. The same is probably true for Bertrand Russell, William Wordsworth, and Gandhi.

Okay, I'm kidding about Gandhi. Golf was never on his radar, as far as I know. But as other writers have pointed out, he said something that would have many golfers nodding in agreement. Gandhi said that he tried to do his work "without fear of failure and without hope of success." If the average weekend player is honest about his or her approach to the game, those words might be embroidered on the old golf bag.

Gandhi's quote, like many others in this book, gets to the heart of the conflicting emotions this game can produce. One minute you're beaming with ridiculous pride as your drive screams down the center of the fairway; the next you're looking for the nearest tree to wrap your 9-iron around, after dropping your approach shot into the drink. From sublime happiness to the darkest rage, all within the space of a few minutes. It only makes sense because, as Arnold Daly said, "Golf is like a love affair. If you don't take it seriously, it's not fun; if you do take it seriously, it breaks your heart.

Nearly everyone quoted in this book expresses a deep and abiding love for golf—unless they're complaining about how the game has the power to make them feel helpless and incompetent. It's this dichotomy that makes the wisdom collected here so endlessly entertaining. I hope you enjoy reading the book as much as I've enjoyed pulling it together.

—Niels Aaboe
New York City

CREDIT: Craig O'Neal

PART ONE

How To

*Each player must accept the
cards life deals him or her,
but once they are in hand, he or
she alone must decide
how to play the cards in order to
win the game.*
—VOLTAIRE

If a ball be stop'd by any person, horse, dog or anything else, the ball so stop'd must be played where it lyes.
—RULE NUMBER X OF THE LEITH CODE, 1744, SCOTLAND

• • •

Golf may be played anywhere—that is, anywhere where there is room, but the quality of golf will depend upon the kind of place it is played on, and the manner which the land is laid out and kept.
—GARDEN SMITH, 1898

• • •

This invention relates to balls such as are used in the game of golf, and has for its object to improve the flight of the ball in the air, and its action on the ground.
—EXCERPT FROM WILLIAM TAYLOR'S PATENT APPLICATION FOR THE DYMPL BALL, 1905

• • •

One would be remiss if, during any discussion of the advancement in balls and clubs, another invention was not mentioned. That would be the grass mower in the 1850s, which allowed golf to be played on grassland and during the growing season for grass.
—JOHN JENCHURA, from *GOLF—A GOOD WALK AND THEN SOME*

• • •

The secret of being able to hit a golf ball a very long way is freedom of action and the application of strength.
—HAROLD HORSFALL HILTON, *MODERN GOLF*

• • •

The secret of golf is to turn three shots into two.
—BOBBY JONES

• • •

The game, unlike tennis, squash, pinochle, chess, *boccie*, and practically every other competitive joust, is not played on the same dull rectangle or board or in the identical pit or valley the world over but is played across delightful varieties of open landscape.
—ALISTAIR COOK, *GOLF: THE MARVELOUS MANIA*

• • •

Sometimes thinking too much can destroy your momentum.
—*TOM WATSON*

• • •

They say "practice makes perfect." Of course, it doesn't. For the vast majority of golfers it merely consolidates imperfection.
—*HENRY LONGHURST*

• • •

It is good sportsmanship to not pick up lost golf balls while they are still rolling.
—*MARK TWAIN*

• • •

It's not artificial and no tricks about it. Either you hit the fairway or you're going to be in trouble.
—*MIKE WEIR*

• • •

How To

Try to think where you want to put the ball, not where you don't want it to go.
—*Billy Casper*

• • •

You must play boldly to win.
—Arnold Palmer

• • •

Don't be in such a hurry. That little white ball isn't going to run away from you.
—*Patty Berg*

• • •

My earnest advice to the beginner is—betake yourself to a tutor of some kind . . . and set yourself on the right path at the beginning of your journey. You have a long, hard road to travel, and a good start will mean a lot to you as time goes on.
—Henry Longhurst, from *On Taking Lessons*

• • •

CREDIT: Comstock

When I am asked, "What is your advice for getting out from behind a tree?", I generally reply, "My advice is not to get behind a tree in the first place."
—REX LARDNER, FROM *OUT OF THE BUNKER AND INTO THE TREES*

• • •

Having a clear image of your swing's ultimate destination can significantly improve the quality of the moves that get you there.
—NICK FALDO, FROM *A SWING FOR LIFE*

• • •

An efficient golf swing incorporates the fewest moving parts while producing maximum results in terms of direction, distance, and ball flight. These factors add up to control, and to me the ultimate art of golf is in controlling the ball.
—NICK PRICE, FROM *THE SWING: MASTERING THE PRINCIPLES OF THE GAME*

• • •

Most golfers come to the first tee uncommitted to anything except looking good and not being embarrassed. If this is your only commitment, I can guarantee you that your golfing experience will be erratic and often filed with anxiety.
—FRED SHOEMAKER, FROM *EXTRAORDINARY GOLF*

• • •

The only two golf tips I have found consistently useful are these. One (from Jack Nicklaus) on long putts, think of yourself putting the ball half the distance and having it roll the rest of the way. Two (from I forget—Mac Divot?): on chip shots, to keep from underhitting, imagine yourself *throwing* the ball to the green with the right hand.
—JOHN UPDIKE

• • •

There is no movement in the golf swing so difficult that cannot be made even more difficult by careful study and diligent practice.
—THOMAS BOSWELL

• • •

You must work very hard to become a natural golfer.
—GARY PLAYER

• • •

There is no such thing as a born golfer.
—BEN HOGAN

• • •

Make the basic shot-making decision early, clearly and firmly,
and then ritualize all the necessary acts of preparation.
—SAM SNEAD

• • •

My father tells me to "grip the seven-iron like you're holding a
bird in your hands and don't want to crush it."
—STEVE FRIEDMAN

• • •

The formula for success is simple: practice and concentration,
then more practice and more concentration.
—BABE DIDRIKSON ZAHARIAS

• • •

Never try to keep more than 300 separate thoughts in your mind during your swing.
—HENRY BEARD

• • •

For the ambitious golfer, I do strongly urge regular practice sessions, and all of them with a definite purpose or intent.
—BOB CHARLES, FROM *LEFT-HANDED GOLF*

• • •

It's not enough to swing at the ball. You've got to loosen your girdle and really let the ball have it.
—BABE DIDRIKSON ZAHARIAS

• • •

There is, and always will be, room for improvement.
—TIGER WOODS

• • •

CREDIT: iStockphoto/Thinkstock

Michelle Wie   CREDIT: Keith Allison from Owings Mills, USA

It's like a machine—you want as few moving parts as possible in order to avoid breaking down.
—TOM LEHMAN

• • •

No golfer can ever become too good to practice.
—MAY HEZLET

• • •

The practice area is golf's real incubator. It is there that questions about the mechanics of the game are answered, experiments are proved or disproved, swings are grooved, and confidence restored.
—BOB CHARLES, FROM *LEFT-HANDED GOLF*

• • •

In baseball you hit your home runs over the right-field fence, the left-field fence, the center-field fence. Nobody cares. In golf everything has got to be over second base.
—KEN HARRELSON, FORMER ALL-STAR AND PGA PRO

• • •

The reason why the pro tells you to keep your head down is so you can't see him laughing.
—PHYLLIS DILLER

• • •

How do you expect to ever be a pro with that left elbow coming out like that?
—THE HEAD PRO AT A LOCAL COUNTRY CLUB TO A YOUNG SAM SNEAD

• • •

The next thing I learned was to trust my own game. If anybody ever offered to "fix" what was wrong with me, why, I was gonna run for the hills.
—SAM SNEAD

• • •

You see that practice ground out there? It is an evil place. It's full of so-called coaches waiting to pounce on young guys or players who have lost their form. They just hope they can make money out of them.
—ERNIE ELS

• • •

Ernie Els

CREDIT: billypoonphotos

I know I'm getting better at golf because I'm hitting fewer spectators.
—GERALD FORD

• • •

There is no such thing as a natural touch. Touch is something you create by hitting millions of golf balls.
—LEE TREVINO

• • •

I never practice golf. All it does is louse up my game.
—ORVILLE MOODY

• • •

I used to go to the bar when I finished a round. These kids today go back and practice.
—LEE TREVINO

• • •

When I started out, you'd finish your round and have a scotch or two with some of the other players. Today, if you run into another player after a round, you give them a Power Bar and a glass of carrot juice.
—AMY ALCOTT

• • •

Golfers tend to practice the things they're already good at.
—TOM WEISKOPF

• • •

If you can't putt, you can't play. It's as simple as that.
—FREDDIE BENNETT, AUGUSTA NATIONAL CADDY MASTER

• • •

Selecting a putter is like selecting a wife. To each his own.
—BEN HOGAN

• • •

It is often said that if a golfer's mind is somewhere else while he is playing, it will show up most clearly in his putting.
—GARY PLAYER

• • •

CREDIT: Stockbyte

The easiest shot in golf is the fourth putt.
—Ring Lardner

• • •

Seeing [the doctor] standing tensely over four-foot putts, I reflected that if he held his scalpel with as much apprehension and self-doubt as his putter, I'd never want to be on his operating table.
—W. Timothy Gallwey, from *The Inner Game of Golf*

• • •

Golf, like measles, should be caught young, for, if postponed to riper years, the results may be serious.
—P.G. Wodehouse

• • •

Who cares whether the head case who dreamed the whole thing up was a Scottish whackjob, a Dutch whackjob, or a Chinese whackjob? We still have to figure out how to slash the ball out of hip-high rough, or blast a sand shot from an unraked footprint in the bunker, or hit a duffed drive off the ladies tee with dignity.
—Henry Beard, from *Golf: An Unofficial and Unauthorized History of the World's Most Preposterous Sport*

• • •

Thinking without acting is the number-one golf disease.
—SAM SNEAD

• • •

Remember you have to be comfortable. Golf is not a life or death situation. It's just a game and should be treated as such. Stay loose.
—CHI-CHI RODRIQUEZ

• • •

Whenever I play, I try to do my absolute best. Knowing during those four days there will be ups and downs. Part of those time, I have a feeling like I can win and I always draw on that feeling.
—TOM WATSON

• • •

Anxiety under pressure has driven a lot of golfers out of the game. They're people you don't know of and never heard about because they couldn't handle it. That includes some very talented guys.
—JIM MCLEAN, INSTRUCTOR TO VARIOUS TOURING PROS

• • •

CREDIT: iStockphoto/Thinkstock

The average golfer can feel his hands tremble just standing over a 4-foot putt to win a weekend match, and for them, all that's at stake is their ego.
—JOE PARENT, PSYCHOLOGIST AND AUTHOR OF *ZEN OF GOLF*

• • •

I was just thinking about my health, one shot at a time, one hole at a time.
—CHARLIE BELJAN, WHO WON THE 2012 CHILDREN'S MIRACLE NETWORK HOSPITALS CLASSIC DESPITE SUFFERING A SEVERE PANIC ATTACK

• • •

Confidence is the most important single factor in this game, and no matter how great your natural talent, there is only one way to obtain and sustain it: work.
—JACK NICKLAUS

• • •

Each of us is our own judge, jury and executioner.
—GREG NORMAN, AFTER HE DISQUALIFIED HIMSELF FROM
THE 1996 GREATER HARTFORD OPEN BECAUSE OF A MIX-UP
OVER THE BALLS HE USED

• • •

There is only one way to play the game. You might as well praise
a man for not robbing a bank.
—BOBBY JONES, AFTER HE WAS PRAISED FOR PENALIZING
HIMSELF FOR MOVING HIS BALL MARKER

• • •

I've been told the story of one golfer who got so tired of con-
stantly being asked what club he used on his shots that he
ordered a set of irons all marked with the same number: eight!
—SIR BOB CHARLES

• • •

Forget your opponents. Always play against par.
—SAM SNEAD

• • •

Gary Player   CREDIT: Lady 11390

"Par" is an example of an illusory "box" that mid- to high-hand-icap golfers create for themselves. They would do well to think outside of it.
—JOSEPH PARENT, FROM *THE ZEN OF GOLF*

• • •

You can be the greatest iron player in the world or the greatest putter, but if you can't get the ball in position to use your great-ness, you can't win.
—BEN HOGAN

• • •

It has been an extremely pleasant and rewarding collaboration for those of us who were privileged to work with Ben Hogan. My only personal regret has been that my friends' golf games have improved as much as my own.
—HERBERT WARREN WIND

• • •

The only thing you should force in a golf swing is the club back in
the bag.
—BYRON NELSON

• • •

Around the clubhouse they'll tell you that even God has to practice his putting. In fact, even Nicklaus does.
—JIM MURRAY

• • •

I open the driving range and I close it. I thought you ought to
know that I work hard. I like practicing. I enjoy it. If I did not
enjoy it I wouldn't do it.
—VIJAY SINGH

• • •

A driving range is the place where golfers go to get all the good shots out of their system.
—HENRY BEARD

• • •

I spent an hour in the mud with my sand wedge, creating lies where the ball was submerged or half-submerged, plugged or sitting up on the mud. I came out of there looking like a mud wrestler, but I learned an awful lot. So practice when it's wet once in a while. You'll pick up things you'll never forget.
—RAYMOND FLOYD

• • •

Golf is primarily a fight with oneself. In a strong personality the battle is more hotly contested, of course, than in a person of anemic character.
—REX LARDNER, FROM *OUT OF THE BUNKER AND INTO THE TREES*

• • •

The best place to refine your swing is, of course, on the practice range. You will have the opportunity to make the same mistakes over and over again so that you no longer have to think about them, and they become part of your game.
—STEPHEN BAKER

• • •

It may not be out of place here to say that I never won a major championship until I learned to play golf against something, not somebody. And that something was par.
—BOBBY JONES

• • •

My approach to golf is that I always play to beat the course.
—BOBBY LOCKE, FROM *ON GOLF*

• • •

CREDIT: iStockphoto\Thinkstock

A golfer . . . must say to the ball, 'Go to that spot.' The best players who ever played must have thought that way, *willing* the ball there, you see.
—ARNOLD PALMER

• • •

I'm going to give you a little advice. There's a force in the universe that makes things happen. And all you have to do is get in touch with it, stop thinking, let things happen, and be the ball.
—CHEVY CHASE AS TY WEBB IN *CADDYSHACK*

• • •

The higher you hit the ball, the harder it lands, and the harder it lands, the more unpredictable the bounce.
—RAYMOND FLOYD

• • •

How To

My body knows how to play golf. I've trained it to do that. It's just a matter of keeping my conscious mind out of it.
—TIGER WOODS

• • •

Placing the ball in the right position for the next shot is eighty percent of winning.
—BEN HOGAN

• • •

Inside each and every one of us is our one, true authentic swing. Something we was born with. Something that's ours and ours alone. Something that can't be learned . . . something that's got to be remembered.
—WILL SMITH AS BAGGER VANCE IN *THE LEGEND OF BAGGER VANCE*

• • •

Take dead aim.
—HARVEY PENICK, FROM HIS *LITTLE RED BOOK*

• • •

Read it, roll it, hole it.
—JOSH FLITTER AS EDDIE LOWERY IN *THE GREATEST GAME EVER PLAYED*

• • •

There are no short hitters on tour anymore—just long and unbelievably long.
—SAM SNEAD

• • •

I just hit it hard as I can, and if I find the ball, I hit it again.
—JOHN DALY

• • •

I can airmail the golf ball, but sometimes I don't put the right address on it.
—JIM DENT

• • •

How To

The player of the present day is a longer driver than the player of
the past generation, for he has found out that it is quite possible
to hit the ball very hard and still cause it to fly comparatively
straight.
—Harold Horsfall Hilton, from *Modern Golf*

• • •

If Jack Nicklaus had to play my tee shots he couldn't break 80.
He'd be running a string of drug stores in Ohio.
—Lee Trevino

• • •

Ninety percent of putts that are short don't go in.
—Yogi Berra

• • •

All there is to putting is keeping the head steady and the face of the putter moving squarely across the line to the hole. The problem is there are at least a thousand ways of doing those two things.
—TOMMY ARMOUR

• • •

The putter is a club designed . . . to hit the ball partway to the hole.
—REX LARDNER

• • •

It is an axiom of the game that more matches are won and lost on the green than anywhere else.
—HAROLD HORSFALL HILTON, *THE MODERN GAME*

• • •

There have been many players who stroke the ball incredibly well and haven't had a tremendous career because of a lack of a short game.
—PHIL MICKELSON

• • •

That little white ball won't move until you hit it, and there's nothing you can do after it has gone.
—BABE DIDRIKSON ZAHARIAS

• • •

One week you've discovered the secret to the game; the next week you never want to play it again.
—JOHN FEINSTEIN, FROM *A GOOD WALK SPOILED*

• • •

Every day I tell myself this is going to be fun today. I try to put myself in a great frame of mind before I go out—then I screw it up with the first shot.
—JOHNNY MILLER

• • •

Bubba Watson

CREDIT: Hone Morihana

The only thing you can learn from golf books is that you can't learn anything from golf books, but you have to read an awful lot of golf books to learn it.
—HENRY BEARD, FROM *MULLIGAN'S LAWS*

• • •

I just play golf. I attack. I always attack. I don't like to go to the center of the greens. I want to hit the incredible shot; who doesn't? That's why we play the game of golf, to pull off the amazing shot.
—BUBBA WATSON

• • •

It's easy to become a great golfer, if you have a strong golf education.
—JIRO NAKAZAKI, PGA GOLF PROFESSIONAL AND A FULL-TIME GOLF INSTRUCTOR AND BLOGGER WITH A BACKGROUND IN PSYCHOLOGY

• • •

I never lose my temper with an opponent. I was angry only with myself. It always seemed . . . such an utterly useless and idiotic thing to stand up to a perfectly simple shot, one that I know I can make a hundred times running without a miss—and then mess up the blamed thing, the one time I want to make it! . . . I think it was Stevenson who said that bad men and fools eventually got what was coming to them, but the fools first.
—BOBBY JONES, FROM *DOWN THE FAIRWAY*

• • •

Golf is the most difficult game in the world . . . The margin for error is minimal.
—GARY PLAYER

• • •

It's as easy to reduce your handicap as it is to reduce your hat size.
—HENRY BEARD, FROM *MULLIGAN'S LAWS*

• • •

If you're going to throw a club in temper, it's important to throw it ahead of you in the direction of the green. That way you don't waste energy going back to pick it up.
—Tommy Bolt

• • •

Tommy Bolt's putter has spent more time in the air than Lindbergh.
—Jimmy Demaret

• • •

You must accept your disappointments and triumphs equally.
—Harvey Penick, from his *Little Red Book*

• • •

Ultimately, you must have the heart and head to play a shot and the courage to accept the consequences.
—Tiger Woods

• • •

CREDIT: Metallion

PART TWO

Wherefore

Those who dare to fail miserably
can achieve greatly.
—JOHN F. KENNEDY

Golf: A game in which you claim the privileges of age, and retain the playthings of childhood.
—SAMUEL JOHNSON

• • •

When Scotland gave to England the rather dubious blessing of her Scottish kings, she gave therewith a gift which was an undoubted boon: the game of golf
—HORACE G. HUTCHINSON, GOLF:
A COMPLETE HISTORY (1905)

• • •

I was shown one particular set of golfers, the youngest of whom was turned of fourscore. They were all gentlemen of independent fortunes, who had amused themselves with this pastime for the best part of a century, without ever having felt the least alarm from sickness or disgust; and they never went to bed without having each the best part of a gallon of claret in his belly.
—HUMPHREY CLINKER, 1771

• • •

Wherefore

CREDIT: Thomas Northcutt

Golf is so popular simply because it is the best game in the world at which to be bad.
—A.A. MILNE

• • •

A: "Is golf any use? That's what I'm asking you. Can you name me a single case where devotion to this pestilential game has done a man any practical good?"
B: "I could name a thousand."
—P.G. WODEHOUSE, FROM *THE CLICKING OF CUTHBERT*

• • •

To dwell near a golf course and work hard at the game; to go away whenever the spirit moved one . . . to some paradise by the seas with a pleasant companion or two; to stay as long as one liked . . . even to think of it is still to feel faintly the old desire.
—BERNARD DARWIN

• • •

When I was a young player, my dream was to own a ranch. Golf was the only way I was going to get that ranch. And every tournament I played in, I was going after a piece of it. . . . That was what I won tournaments for.
—Byron Nelson

• • •

Golf is a compromise between what your ego wants you to do, what experience tells you to do, and what your nerve lets you do.
—Bruce Crampton

• • •

In golf, as in no other sport, your principal opponent is yourself. No one touches the golfer's ball but the golfer himself. If you slice your approach with your 5-iron into a luxurious patch of brier, you cannot slink out of responsibility for a rotten shot by turning to your adversary, as you can in tennis, and exclaiming, "Beautiful shot, Reg!"
—Herbert Warren Wind

• • •

CREDIT: iStockphoto/Thinkstock

There is something tonic and bracing about the fact that you are totally responsible for the fate of the little white ball and that you have only one chance of hitting it correctly (there is no second serve, no third strike, no fourth down, etc.).
—ALISTAIR COOKE, *GOLF: THE MARVELOUS MANIA*

• • •

There are times when I am convinced that I actually know something about playing the irons—almost.
—BOBBY JONES

• • •

That's the way it is. Just when you get ready to give up, something wonderful happens.
—BILL CLINTON

• • •

We're not out there throwing grass up in the air, testing the winds. We like to bang away.
—GEORGE W. BUSH, ON HOW HE AND HIS FATHER PLAY GOLF

• • •

Anyone who knows Dan [Quayle] knows that he would rather play golf than have sex, any day.
—MARILYN QUAYLE

• • •

I've never found sex that exciting, not nearly as exciting as golf.
—DAVE HILL

• • •

Such a pure feeling is the well-struck golf shot.
—KEVIN COSTNER AS ROY 'TIN CUP' MCAVOY IN TIN CUP

• • •

Though [the average golfer] enjoys the fun of hitting the ball
he values the game largely for the exercise it gives him and the
pleasant social intercourse afforded by the nineteenth hole, where
his conversation turns on motor cars, his day's play, the Minister
of Transport—and his day's play.
—HENRY LONGHURST, THE EVENING STANDARD (1934)

• • •

Why do people play golf? Oddly enough, they play it to destroy
themselves. Once this premise is accepted, golf can be an interesting and occasionally pleasant game.
—REX LARDNER, FROM OUT OF THE ROUGH AND INTO THE
TREES

• • •

It is almost impossible to remember how tragic a place the world
is when playing golf.
—ROBERT WILSON LYND

• • •

Golf gives you an insight into human nature, your own as well as your opponents. Eighteen holes of match or medal play will teach you more about your foe than will 18 years of dealing with him across a desk.
—GRANTLAND RICE

• • •

With a fine sea view, and a clear course in front of him, the golfer should find no difficulty in dismissing all worries from his mind, and regarding golf, even if it be very indifferent golf, as the true and adequate end of a man's existence.
—ARTHUR BALFOUR

• • •

It is a great thing to have your holes well guarded with hazards on the hither and farther sides and round about them.
—HORACE G. HUTCHINSON, GOLF:
THE COMPLETE GAME (1905)

• • •

Wherefore

CREDIT: Alan Stewart

51

The beauty of golf, you're in charge out here.
—Mike Weir

• • •

The joy of driving a ball straight after a week of slicing, the joy of putting a mashie shot dead, the joy of even a moderate stroke with a brassie; best of all, the joy of the perfect cleek shot—these things the good player will never know. Every stroke we bad players make we make in hope.
—A.A. Milne, from *The Charm of Golf*

• • •

Don't be tense. Don't try to just hammer the ball. And, most of all, don't worry. Often people in Pro-Ams are so nervous that they top the ball, or worse, they play an air shot. Remember, at the end of the day, golf is a game to be enjoyed.
—Marie-Laure de Lorenzi

• • •

Re-reading these pieces [written about golf] has had, then, for
me, a bitter flavor of the valedictory. Beneath their comedy of
complaints there ran always a bubbling undercurrent of hope, of
a tomorrow when the skies would be utterly blue and the swing
equally pure.
—JOHN UPDIKE, FROM THE PREFACE TO GOLF DREAMS

• • •

It's a cruel game sometimes. It's a cruel game.
—TOM KITE

• • •

There is no comfort zone in golf.
—TIGER WOODS

• • •

I don't like when people cheer me. I like it better when they cheer
against me.
—SEVE BALLESTEROS

• • •

CREDIT: Thomas Northcutt

Golf is played by twenty million mature American men whose
wives think they are out having fun.
—JIM BISHOP

• • •

Golf is the loneliest of all games, not excluding postal chess.
—PETER DOBEREINER

• • •

Golf is a very personal game in which each player is hostage to
his own incompetence. Sure, a golfer may strive for conviviality
as he and his comrades scour ankle deep for the orphaned golf
ball . . . [But] the transient exhilaration of a cleanly hit four iron,
or the profound misery of a shanked wedge shot . . . is ultimately
unshared.
—WILLIAM HALLBERG, FROM PERFECT LIES

• • •

There are few experiences in sport that can compare with the thrill that the average golfer or the skillful golfer receives when he plays a famous course for he first time.
—HERBERT WARREN WIND, FROM *FOLLOWING THROUGH*

• • •

I didn't get turned on to playing [golf] until 10 or 12 years ago. Sometime after the advent of Tiger Woods.
—MORGAN FREEMAN

• • •

Golf combines two favorite American pastimes: taking long walks and hitting things with a stick.
—P.J. O'ROURKE

• • •

Golf is not an exact science. Einstein was lousy at it.
—BOB TOSKI

• • •

For me, the worst part of playing golf, by far, has always been hitting the ball.
—DAVE BARRY

• • •

It's much better when a celebrity wins rather than a Fortune 500 guy. It's the slobs versus the snobs.
—GEORGE LOPEZ, ON THE PEBBLE BEACH PRO-AM

• • •

It's just *golf*. It's not life and death.
—PAUL AZINGER

• • •

It's nice to be a good golfer and win championships, but hell, being the finest golfer in the world never cured anyone of polio.
—TOMMY ARMOUR

• • •

I don't know very much. I know a little bit about golf. I know how to make a stew. And I know how to be a decent man.
—BYRON NELSON

• • •

Golf is all about the bounce-back stat. Actually, life is all about the bounce-back stat.
—STUART APPLEBY

• • •

Do your best one shot at a time and then move on. Remember that golf is just a game.
—NANCY LOPEZ

• • •

Golf is a very difficult game to play to a high standard, but it is one of the easiest games to play well enough to enjoy. After all, the ball is stationary. You don't need much natural reflex ability or great strength to see you through.
—PETER ALLIS, FROM GOLF:
THE CURE FOR A GRUMPY OLD MAN

• • •

CREDIT: iStockphoto/Thinkstock

Golf is a game in which players lie about their scores to people who used to be their friends after a day spent thrashing about on surfaces that look like spoiled pastures. That's why we take it up 'for the good of our health.'
—KAREN DURASH

• • •

I've learned there are no absolutes in golf. You name me a player that does it one way. I'll name you one just as successful who does the opposite.
—GARY PLAYER

• • •

Losing your temper doesn't get you anywhere at golf. It only spoils your next shot.
—P.G. WODEHOUSE, FROM *GOLF WITHOUT TEARS*

• • •

I'm excited, I'm almost seventy and I'm gonna go practice.
—Lee Trevino's reaction after Tom Watson held
the 2009 British Open lead after two rounds at age
fifty-nine

• • •

When you play professional golf you lose the ability to play
simply for fun. If I'm playing a practice round, and I hit a 2-iron
just perfectly, I don't get a buzz. I get nothing. Unless it happens
in a tournament, in a competition, I get nothing.
—Peter Teravainen

• • •

I found I can still play, and I also found that I can make bad
swings with the driver when I lose my focus. I'll treat the Champions Tour as a bonus where the stress is not as high.
—Ian Baker-Finch

• • •

Why quit? Your clubs have no idea how old you are.
—Lee Trevino

• • •

The golfer is never old until he is decrepit. So long as Providence allows his the use of two legs active enough to carry him round the green, and two arms supple enough to take a 'half swing,' there is no reason why his enjoyment of the game need be seriously diminished.
—Arthur Balfour

• • •

The trouble about reaching 92 is that regrets for a misspent life are bound to creep in, and whenever you see me with a furrowed brow you can be sure that what is on my mind is the thought that if only I had taken up golf earlier . . . I might have got my handicap down to under 18.
—P.G. Wodehouse

• • •

It's such an amazing feeling, playing among golf's best.
—MATT KUCHAR

• • •

No, no, don't think of it as work—the whole point is just to enjoy yourself.
—TIM MATHESON AS OTTER DURING THE GOLF SCENE IN *ANIMAL HOUSE*

• • •

I am . . . much more comfortable on the golf course than perhaps anyplace else.
—TIGER WOODS

• • •

I never thought of myself as anything less than a winner.
—PATTI SHEEHAN

• • •

Sergio Garcia

CREDIT: Usien

When you start driving your ball down the middle, you meet a
different class of people.
—PHIL HARRIS

• • •

Hit the ball up to the hole . . . You meet a better class of person
up there.
—BEN HOGAN

• • •

I hit it again because that shot was a defining moment, and when
a defining moment comes along, you define the moment . . . or
the moment defines you.
—KEVIN COSTNER AS ROY 'TIN CIP' MCAVOY IN *TIN CUP*

• • •

In my fifty-seven years of golf, this hole in one is my first ever. To
think how many balls I have hit in my life—I was running out of
time.
—LOUISE SUGGS

• • •

I've thrown clubs. I launched my 7-iron and managed to get it stuck in a tree. All my buddies were laughing because they know how competitive I am. They love torturing me in the only sport I can't beat them.
—MICHAEL PHELPS

• • •

Murphy's Law and quantum physics agree that almost nothing in life behaves as you'd like it to—not children, politicians, or pets, and least of all a small white ball destined for a distant hole in the ground.
—CHARLES LINDSAY, FROM LOST BALLS, GREAT HOLES

• • •

The inexhaustible competitive charm of golf, for the non-professional player, lies in its handicap strokes, whereby all players are theoretically equalized and an underdog can become, with a small shift of fortunes, a top dog.
—JOHN UPDIKE, FROM THE CAMARADERIE OF GOLF II

• • •

Golf is merely an expensive way of leaving home.
—Michael Parkinson

• • •

The perfectionist who tries to play golf for a living usually ends up saying to hell with it. . . . Perfectionists are determined to master things, and you can never master golf.
—Tom Weiskopf

• • •

I've always had three rules for playing well on the tour: no pushups, no swimming, and no sex after Wednesday.
—Sam Snead

• • •

Golf is my boyfriend right now.
—KARRIE WEBB

• • •

When u run out of balls u run out of balls.
—JOHN DALY, IN A TWEET AFTER WITHDRAWING FROM THE
2011 AUSTRALIAN OPEN DURING THE FIRST ROUND

• • •

Karrie Webb

CREDIT: Keith Allison

Bobby Jones

CREDIT: Onbekend

PART THREE

The Players

*When love and skill work
together, expect a masterpiece.*
—John Ruskin

Walter Hagen is happiest when there's a hard battle ahead and he
must come from behind to win.
—GRANTLAND RICE

• • •

All the professionals who go after the big money today should say
a silent thanks to Walter Hagen each time they stretch a check
between their fingers. It was Walter who made professional golf
what it is.
—GENE SARAZEN

• • •

Golf without [Bobby] Jones would be like France without Paris—
leaderless, lightless and lonely.
—HERBERT WARREN WIND

• • •

Here you are, the greatest golfer in the world being introduced by the worst one.
—New York City Mayor Jimmy Walker to Bobby Jones, 1930

• • •

Byron (Nelson) had the kind of game he could park like a fine automobile. There weren't a lot of moving parts and the engine was beautifully tuned. That's why he could leave the game for whole periods of time, then come back to play outstandingly well with only a little practice.
—Eddie Merrins

• • •

Would I trade all my slicing arcs and all my hooking swerves for Byron Nelson's perfect play? You bet your shirt I would.
—Grantland Rice

• • •

Byron didn't smoke, didn't drink, didn't play around, didn't dance, and I wondered just what the hell he does do.
—Sam Snead

• • •

[Ben Hogan] sought out tour friends that had 'personality' because he felt that he didn't. He thought he could only talk with his golf clubs.
—Dan Jenkins

• • •

Every time I watch Ben Hogan hit a golf ball, I learn something.
—Bob Toksi

• • •

Nobody gets close to Ben Hogan.
—Jimmy Demaret

• • •

Nobody in the pro ranks outputts Hogan.
—SHIRLEY POVICH

• • •

Ben Hogan would rather let a black widow spider crawl around
inside his shirt than hit a hook.
—CLAUDE HARMON

• • •

Hogan is the most ruthless, most cold-blooded and least compas-
sionate of golf foremen. He doesn't merely want to beat you. He
wants to trample you underfoot.
—LAWTON CARVER, INDEPENDENT NEWS SERVICE

• • •

[Jimmy Demaret] was the most underrated golfer in history. This man played shots I haven't even dreamed of. I learned them. But it was Jimmy who showed them to me first.
—BEN HOGAN

• • •

I never met one person who said they didn't like Jimmy Demaret.
—SAM SNEAD

• • •

Babe [Zaharias] has now completely outclassed all her challengers. She has set the pattern by which a champion should act on the course and off it and in the future all women golfers must be judged as they measure up to the standard or fail to do so.
—AL LANEY, FROM THE BABE COMES BACK

• • •

The early golf swing was more or less just a swing. Babe [Zaharias] brought the swing and a hit to the game. She got people, especially women, power-minded.
—Patty Berg

• • •

This kid has a perfect swing like Sam Snead—only it's better.
—Gene Sarazan on Gene Littler

• • •

If any one man turned golf from an elitist pastime to one played and watched by millions, that man was Arnold Palmer.
—Peter Alliss, from *Alliss's 19th Hole*

• • •

Arnold Palmer, 1953

CREDIT: U.S. Coast Guard

In a sport that was high society, he made it `High Noon.'
—BROADCASTER VIN SCULLY ON ARNOLD PALMER

• • •

Can you imagine being Arnold Palmer and single?
—A SPECTATOR AT THE 1962 U.S. OPEN

• • •

You made all this possible, Arnold. We're all here because of you.
—ROCCO MEDIATE TO ARNOLD PALMER AFTER PALMER
FINISHED HIS LAST ROUND AT THE 1994 U.S. OPEN

• • •

The two best bad-weather players I ever saw were Tom Watson
and Arnold Palmer. The worse the conditions got, the better they
played.
—GARY PLAYER

• • •

Jack Nicklaus is unique in that he stayed at the peak of the game longer than any other golfer, which is to say that he could stand the heat better.
—FRANK HANNIGAN, *GOLF DIGEST*

• • •

Competing against Jack and Arnold, at our peaks, those were the greatest days of my life. We tried like hell to beat each other.
—GARY PLAYER

• • •

At times we became so hyper about beating each other that we let someone else go right by us and win. But our competition was fun and good for the game.
—ARNOLD PALMER, ON HIS COMPETITION WITH JACK NICKLAUS

• • •

My chances are as good as Jack [Nicklaus's]. The pressure is on him. He's the best ever, the odds-on favorite. If I lose, people expect it. If he loses, it makes me look like a hero.
—LEE TREVINO, BEFORE WINNING THE 1971 U.S. OPEN

• • •

There's about as much chance of someone breaking Nicklaus's Majors record [of 18 wins] as there is somebody winning 11 tournaments in a row like Byron Nelson did.
—MIKE SOUCHAK

• • •

At least for a few short hours, I was seeing the best that ever was playing as good as he could.
—PETER JACOBSEN, ON BEING PAIRED WITH JACK NICKLAUS AT THE 1986 MEMORIAL TOURNAMENT

• • •

[Nicklaus would stand] on that first tee and look at you with those icy blue eyes and you knew that he knew he was going to beat the shit out of you.
—TOM WEISKOPF

• • •

I'm not anywhere close to being Jack Nicklaus, but why not have that as a goal?
—HALE IRWIN

• • •

For some reason or other, Jack Nicklaus always moves one more in defeat than in victory. I don't know why exactly this is, for he is an excellent winner. Anyway, he is probably the best loser in the game.
—HERBERT WARREN WIND, FROM *NICKLAUS AND WATSON AT TURNBERRY*

• • •

Jack Nicklaus, 2006

CREDIT: pocketwiley

You just don't know how good a player you are. You can win anywhere.
—Jack Nicklaus to Lee Trevino

• • •

Tom Watson is unique . . . He may be the only professional golfer who rooted openly for George McGovern in 1972 against Dwight D. Eisenhower's former caddie.
—Dick Shaap, from *Massacre at Winged Foot*

• • •

Hubert [Green] is not a pretty golfer, in other words. But he is among the finest iron players around. There may be no better man in the game with a pitching wedge from 100 yards on in.
—Dan Jenkins

• • •

Billy Casper is perhaps the most under-rated golfer of the past 50 years.
—PETER ALLIS, FROM *PETER ALLISS' GOLF HEROES*

• • •

[Tom] Watson is the finest hitter of the golf ball to come along since Nicklaus's heyday.
—HERBERT WARREN WIND, FROM *FOLLOWING THROUGH*

• • •

She's a machine. She's awesome. I've never played with someone over 18 holes who didn't miss a shot.
—AARON BARBER, AFTER ANNIKA SORENSTAM'S FIRST ROUND PERFORMANCE IN THE 2003 COLONIAL TOURNAMENT, WHERE SHE WAS THE ONLY WOMAN IN THE FIELD

• • •

Annika Sorenstam

CREDIT: Cath Muford

She played amazing. I guess we have the Shark, the Tiger and now we have the Superwoman.
—Jesper Parnevik, on Annika Sorenstam's second round performance in the 2003 Colonial tournament

• • •

The man is an inspiration. Not only is he an example to the weekend hackers and pros ambling towards retirement, he is a reason to take up golf in the first place, for in no other sport is it possible to play, and compete, for so long.
—Paul Forsyth, on fifty-nine-year-old Tom Watson's performance at the 2009 Open Championship

• • •

David Duval is the only person I've heard quote Tennessee Williams and Ayn Rand.
—John Feinstein, From *One on One*

• • •

He could get up and down out of a garbage can. He could do anything with a golf club and a golf ball.
—Jack Nicklaus on Seve Ballesteros

• • •

Best Putter: Ben Crenshaw, who invented the 15-foot gimme.
—Dan Jenkins, from *Fairways and Greens*

• • •

The thing that was phenomenal about Severiano Ballesteros was his imagination and creativity. He saw things that other players don't see. He saw shots they don't see. He was just a genius. He was like watching an artist paint a picture when you'd see him in the trees. I think he was more at home in the trees than in the middle of the fairway. The more trouble he got into, the more comfortable he felt in the situation.
—Butch Harmon

• • •

Greg Norman is like a stretched bow: You draw back the string
and, *foom*, let the arrow go.
—Peter Thomson

• • •

I thought I was playing well and Nick [Price] made me look like a
27-handicapper.
—Greg Norman

• • •

Amy, whatever you do, don't fifteen putt.
—Hollis Stacy to Amy Alcott, who led by nine-shots
as they approached the final green at the 1980
Women's Open

• • •

He just steps up to the ball, takes a deep breath to relax, takes it back, and whomps it. Then he goes and finds it and whomps it again. And when you add up the whomps, the total is usually lower than the other 143 whompers.
—Peter Jacobsen on Fred Couples

• • •

He has two moods 1) annoyed, and 2) about to be annoyed.
—Rick Reilly, writing in Sports Illustrated about Nick Faldo

• • •

The first two or three drives he hit, I wasn't able to see, because the ball came off the club face faster than I was used to.
—Bruce Lietzke, after finishing second to John Daly at the 1991 PGA Championship

• • •

People relate to [John Daly] because he plays golf like they play golf. Grip it, rip it. Hit it, find it. Play like there is no tomorrow.
—Frank Nolilo

• • •

He's longer than Fred Couples. He's longer than Greg Norman.
He's even longer than *War and Peace*.
—Bob Verdi, *Chicago Tribune*, on John Daly

• • •

The intriguing thing about me is I don't know which John Daly
will show up on the golf course.
—John Daly

• • •

[Payne Stewart] was such a competitor. He reminded me of
myself early on. He would make one-line comments to needle
you. If you made one to him, he'd fire one right back at you and
smile. He wasn't looking to outfox you or to con you or to be
malicious. He just had a lot of fun and he had a big heart and a
burning desire to win.
—Jerry Pate

• • •

He seems to have leapfrogged the rest of the field.
—Tom Kite, after Tiger Woods won the 1997 Masters
by 12 strokes

• • •

Tiger has a unique ability to play well when he thinks he's not playing well. I mean, we all kind of smirk and laugh when he says he's got his 'B' game, but that's better than most of our 'A' games.
—Shaun Micheel

• • •

Tiger Woods was playing a different tournament after two rounds. After two rounds, I was playing against everybody else.
—Miquel Angel Jimenez, after finishing second to Tiger Woods in the 2000 U.S. Open, which Woods won by 15 strokes

• • •

Tiger Woods, 1997

CREDIT: Tim Hipps, U.S. Army Family and Morale, Welfare and Recreation Command

Comparing any of us to [Tiger Woods] is like comparing a very, very good painter to Van Gogh or Picasso. He just did things out there none of the rest of us could do. Period.
—DAVID DUVAL

• • •

Tiger has been such a huge hero of mine growing up. To have the opportunity to compete against him, and to beat him sometimes, is quite nice.
—RORY MCILROY

• • •

What Mozart had, we now believe, was the same thing Tiger Woods had—the ability to focus for long periods of time and a father intent on improving his skills.
—DAVID BROOKS

• • •

You can't be more humbled or knocked to your knees than Tiger
is right now, and it's not going to be easy to come back.
—Johnny Miller, on Tiger Woods in 2011

• • •

Now excuse me a moment while I try to envision Ben
Hogan, Arnold Palmer, and Jack Nicklaus playing video
games and eating fruit loops while they try to deal with a
career problem.
—Dan Jenkins

• • •

I would pay any entry fee in the world to watch [Phil] Mickelson
play golf. The man is a true gent and unbelievable to watch. He is
great for golf.
—Touring pro Mark Foster

• • •

Phil Mickelson

CREDIT: minds-eye

That's ridiculous. That's totally ridiculous. That's completely impossible. He'll have to go and have a lie down now.
—Peter Alliss, after Phil Mickelson holed a 100-foot putt

● ● ●

[Michelle Wie] probably has one of the best golf swings I've ever seen, period.
—Davis Love III

● ● ●

When he gets things rolling it's impressive. He's really, really hard to beat.
—Tiger Woods on Rory McIlroy

● ● ●

One of the great things about Rory is that he remains very approachable, very happy-go-lucky, just a normal kid from Northern Ireland with a great talent.
—GRAEME MCDOWELL

• • •

Like everyone else I can see [Rory's] talent and ability. He plays without fear, which is a great way to play.
—PHIL MICKELSON

• • •

Rory McIlroy

CREDIT: Ed (supergolfdude)

CREDIT: Ryan McVay

PART FOUR

The Majors

Old men forget: yet all shall be forgot, But he'll remember with advantages, What feats he did that day.
—WILLIAM SHAKESPEARE, *HENRY V*

CREDIT: pocketwiley

The Masters

[Augusta] can be a very easy course or a very tough one. There isn't a hole out there that can't be birdied if you just think. But there isn't one that can't be double-bogied if you stop thinking.
—BOBBY JONES

• • •

I love this course [Augusta]. I feel I am coming home here. That is why I'm happy. I treat it with respect, like an older person. And sometimes I take a few advantages. But there is always respect.
—SEVE BALLESTEROS

• • •

I enjoy Augusta. I enjoy its challenges. There's no other golf course like this anywhere. Its greens and its challenges on and around the greens are just super, super tough. So the greens are fun to play in sort of a morbid way.
—BEN CRENSHAW

• • •

I have discovered one important thing about the course,
though—those big pine trees don't move.
—FUZZY ZOELLER ON AUGUSTA

• • •

Nothing funny ever happens here at the Masters. Dogs don't bark
and babies don't cry. They wouldn't dare.
—FRANK CHIRKINIAN, CBS SPORTS PRODUCER

• • •

What you find at the Masters is a tournament that is unique
for three main reasons: a uniquely beautiful setting; a course of
uniquely disguised subtlety; and a social occasion civilized more
than the ordinary by the still haunting presence of its founder.
—ALISTAIR COOKE, FROM GOLF: THE MARVELOUS MANIA

• • •

CREDIT: iStockphoto/Thinkstock

Augusta National is like playing a Salvador Dali landscape. I expected a clock to fallout of the trees and hit me in the face.
—David Feherty

• • •

Gene Sarazen's double-eagle [which enabled him to win the 1935 Masters] was a historic shot in the game of golf. And to find somebody of Sarazen's height that could knock it over the water on the green (and in the hole) in two, it's pretty good, isn't it?
—Jack Nicklaus

• • •

It's one thing to say that Doc [Cary Middlecoff] won the 1955 Masters by seven strokes, but it's another to say that he did it by beating Ben Hogan, who was second, and Sam Snead, who was third.
—Dan Jenkins, from Jenkins at the Majors

• • •

On the 15th hole I started thinking about the green jacket. They gave it to Charles Coody.
—JOHNNY MILLER, WHO FINISHED SECOND IN 1971

• • •

I remember the shot at Augusta in 1975 that for much of its flight looked like a double eagle without knickers. This was Jack's 1-iron second shot to the fifteenth in the final round . . . when he was trying to catch and beat Johnny Miller and Tom Weiskopf—and did.
—DAN JENKINS, FROM *FAIRWAYS AND GREENS*

• • •

For an amateur, standing on the first hole at the Masters is the ultimate laxative.
—TREVOR HOMER

• • •

By the time I got to the first tee in my first Masters, I was so scared I could hardly breathe. If you're not a little nervous three, there isn't anything in life that can make you nervous.
—Roger Maltbie

• • •

Augusta . . . reduces putting to something between a lottery and a farce.
—Gary Player

• • •

If you get round it in par, you believe a little bit more in God.
—Dave Marr, when asked why Augusta's 11TH, 12TH, and 13TH holes are known collectively as Amen Corner

• • •

It's a good thing I don't carry a gun.
—Scott Hoch, after he missed a putt that would have won the 1989 Masters

• • •

If I'm going to be honest with myself, the thing I want to do most before I stop playing is win Augusta. I love everything about the tournament.
—Greg Norman, three-time runner up in The Masters

• • •

[A newspaper article] said I was dead, washed-up, through, with no chance of winning again. Oh, I was sizzling. Washed-up, huh?
—Jack Nicklaus, after he won the 1986 Masters at age forty-six

• • •

Hello, you must be Tiger Woods. We've heard a lot about you, and I want to personally welcome you here to Augusta National and the Masters.
—A longtime Augusta member to Vijay Singh in 1995

• • •

CREDIT: pocketwiley

You envision duelling it out with Nicklaus or Watson or Faldo,
but never to do it in the fashion I did.
—TIGER WOODS, AFTER WINNING THE 1997 MASTERS BY 12
STROKES

● ● ●

Leave all the social significance aside. This is like watching Babe
Ruth in the 20s.
—GEORGE WILL, ON TIGER WOODS WINNING THE 1997
MASTERS

● ● ●

[Bubba] Watson's shot to win the Masters was one impressive
professional-level accomplishment. And I didn't even mention
that he got the ball to stop 15 feet from the hole.
—BILL PENNINGTON, THE *NEW YORK TIMES*

● ● ●

I got in these trees and hit a crazy shot and I saw it in my head and somehow I'm here talking to you with a green jacket on.
—BUBBA WATSON, 2012 MASTERS CHAMPION

• • •

The U.S. Open

Any player can win a U.S. Open, but it takes a helluva player to win two.
—WALTER HAGEN

• • •

The U.S. Open is still pure, straight golf, with a minimum of commercial hoopla. In an age where money increasingly dominates all sports, the U.S. Open's single objective remains identifying the best player.
—JACK NICKLAUS, FROM *MY STORY*

• • •

CREDIT: Bernard Gagnon

Unlike the Masters or the British Open, you must hit a lot of fairways and greens [in the U.S. Open], and that was right up my alley.
—Tom Kite

• • •

If the Masters is an offensive show, the U.S. Open is the greatest defensive test in golf.
—Peter Jacobsen

• • •

When you set holes for the U.S. Open, I compare it to driving a race car at the Indy 500. If you're going to win that race you're going to have to drive that car at the very edge, go all out as fast as you can, and you're going to come close to losing it several times if you're going to win it.
—Tom Meeks, the USGA director of rules and competition

• • •

Ask any professional on tour what his five favorite golf courses are in the world, and the one that will be on everyone's list is Pebble Beach.
—TOM WATSON

• • •

As I stood over my ball, suddenly the thought popped into my head of all the times when we were playing as caddies at Glen Gardens and we'd say, "This putt is for the U.S. Open." Now I was really playing that dream out, and it steadied me enough that I sank my putt.
—BYRON NELSON, FROM *HOW I PLAYED THE GAME*

• • •

I'm all right. I'm just happy for my husband. I'm crying with joy.
—VALERIE HOGAN, AFTER BEN HOGAN RETURNED FROM A NEAR-FATAL CAR CRASH AND WON THE 1950 U.S. OPEN AT MERION

• • •

CREDIT: Bert Stewart

I am glad I brought this course, this monster, to its knees.
—BEN HOGAN, AFTER WINNING THE 1951 U.S. OPEN AT
OAKLAND HILLS

• • •

U.S. Open rough, of course, is the great equalizer of the championship. Anybody who misses fairways probably has no chance to contend in the National Championship.
—ARNOLD PALMER, FROM *A GOLFER'S LIFE*

• • •

I need a scythe to play this course.
—JIMMY DEMARET, DURING THE 1950 U.S. OPEN AT MERION

• • •

It's like going back to hell for a second time.
—CHI-CHI RODRIQUEZ, BEFORE THE SECOND ROUND OF THE
1974 U.S. OPEN AT WINGED FOOT

• • •

If Rommel had to deal with furrows like this, he'd never have gotten out of Casablanca.
—JIMMY DEMARET, ON THE BUNKERS AT OAKMONT

• • •

I don't care if they furrow them or not. I don't plan to be in them.
—BEN HOGAN, BEFORE WINNING THE 1953 U.S. OPEN

• • •

Did it ever occur to you that the problem might not be with the bunkers?
—WINGED FOOT ARCHITECT A.W. TILLINGHAST, WHEN TOLD A PLAYER HAD TAKEN FIVE SHOTS TO GET OUT OF ONE

• • •

One of my favorite moments involving mere mortals occurred at the U.S. Open at Medinah outside of Chicago, where Lou Graham and John Mahaffy wound up in an 18-hole playoff.
—DAN JENKINS

• • •

I can see why a defending [U.S.] Open champion never repeats. There is too much commotion around him all week. Too much pressure.
—JOHNNY MILLER

• • •

When people say they dream of playing in the U.S. Open someday, what they're really saying is, they'd like to be good enough to play. Trust me, the U.S. Open is not fun.
—TOM WEISKOPF

• • •

Shoot the lowest score.
—BEN HOGAN'S ADVICE TO NICK FALDO ON HOW TO WIN THE U.S. OPEN

• • •

Two eighty always wins the Open.
—ARNOLD PALMER, BEFORE WINNING HIS FIRST AND ONLY U.S. OPEN CHAMPIONSHIP WITH A SCORE OF 280

• • •

Arnold Palmer won just one U.S. Open [in 1960], but it was a thing of beauty.
—DON WADE, *GOLF DIGEST*

• • •

Mentally, the Open drains you. You've got to have so much patience. You need so much experience to win a tournament like this.
—JOHN DALY

• • •

A [U.S.] Open is never fun. It's a painful test, but you only have to go through it once a year.
—HUBERT GREEN

• • •

All of a sudden I'm an expert on everything. Interviewers want your opinion of golf, foreign policy and even the price of peanuts.
—HUBERT GREEN, THE WINNER IN 1977 AT SOUTHERN HILLS

• • •

CREDIT: Ryan McVay

I've lost the Open a couple of times when I played well enough to win.
—ARNOLD PALMER

• • •

Nobody ever dreamed Hale Irwin would win the 1974 U.S. Open . . . nobody except Hale Irwin.
—HALE IRWIN

• • •

Ask me about my round. I don't want to talk about Tiger Woods [then an amateur].
—TOM WATSON TO A REPORTER, AFTER THE FIRST ROUND OF THE 1996 U.S. OPEN

• • •

[USGA officials] are the genteel clubmen—bankers, businessmen, lawyers—one usually sees at an Open standing among wheat or anthills discussing the fate of another fellow in floral double knit and lime polyester.
—DAN JENKINS (1977)

• • •

Am I far enough ahead that I can choke and still win?
—Lee Trevino to fans during the last round of his
1968 victory at Oak Hill

• • •

I never thought I'd say this, but I'm glad Payne won that now.
It was a very difficult loss to accept, but I expect to have a lot
of opportunities [to win a U.S. Open]. That was his last one. It
makes losing that tournament a little easier now.
—Phil Mickelson, on his one-stroke loss to Payne
Stewart in the 1999 U.S. Open at Pinehurst. Stewart
was killed in a plane crash four months later

• • •

I may buy the Alamo and give it back to Mexico.
—Lee Trevino, when asked what he would do with
the prize money for winning the U.S. Open

• • •

Eighteenth green at St. Andrews

CREDIT: Keith Duff

People talk about me being the leading money winner all the time, but I guarantee you what I most want to be remembered for right now is winning the U.S. Open.
—Tom Kite, after winning the 1992 U.S. Open

• • •

The Open Championship

In Great Britain in recent years the Open Championship has invariably fallen to big physiqued men. Players who are representative of the accurate, scientific type of player, have a habit of finishing in the second position.
—Harold Horsfall Hilton, *Modern Golf*

• • •

In the United States . . . our courses are constructed—fairways blasted through hillsides, streams diverted to fit the strategy of the approach shot, greens built to order by bulldozers. The Old Course [St. Andrews] wasn't made. It was always there.
—Herbert Warren Wind, from *St. Andrews: The Cradle of Golf*

• • •

This is the origin of the game, golf in its purest form, and it's still played that way on a course seemingly untouched by time. Every time I play here, it reminds me that this is still a game.
—ARNOLD PALMER, ON THE OLD COURSE AT ST. ANDREWS

• • •

For some evil reason, some death wish that perhaps is concealed within all of us, the first thing a touring golfer is captivated by in Scotland is the plant life adjacent to all fairways. The heather, whin, bracken, and broom.
—DAN JENKINS

• • •

When the British Open is in Scotland, there's something special about it. And when it's at St. Andrews, it's even greater.
—JACK NICKLAUS

• • •

Any golfer worth his salt has to cross the sea and try to win the British Open.
—JACK NICKLAUS

• • •

First hole at the Old Course, St. Andrews   CREDIT: Keith Duff

There's just something about this golf course I love.
—JOHN DALY, ON ST. ANDREW'S

• • •

To me the Open is the tournament I would come to if I had to
leave a month before and swim over.
—LEE TREVINO

• • •

I turned my back on you, Walter, because a guy with that much
confidence would be fool lucky enough to make it.
—BOBBY JONES TO WALTER HAGEN, AFTER HAGEN NEARLY
MADE AN EAGLE 2 ON THE FINAL HOLE OF THE 1926 OPEN
CHAMPIONSHIP

• • •

I'll be back, even if I have to swim across.
—Gene Sarazan, after he failed to qualify for the 1923 Open

• • •

If there's any one thing I want to accomplish in golf, it's to win the British Open.
—Gene Sarazan to Walter Hagen, before Sarazan won the 1932 Open

• • •

If I could make a pact with the devil I'd take a British Open and happily retire the next day.
—Raymond Floyd

• • •

CREDIT: iStockphoto/Thinkstock

Anytime you're playing golf outside the United States, hell, it's
just camping out.
—SAM SNEAD

• • •

Sam Snead flew to St. Andrews expressly for the 1946 British
Open, took one look at the course, asked if he were in the right
town, and, finding that he was, wanted to fly right back again.
Sam stayed on and proceeded to win that championship. . . .
—HERBERT WARREN WIND, FROM ST. ANDREWS: THE
CRADLE OF GOLF

• • •

He made fifty pounds off that ball—more than I made for win-
ning the Open.
—SAM SNEAD, WHOSE OPEN CADDIE SOLD SNEAD'S WINNING
BALL

• • •

The ball was in a mixture of brambles, wild strawberry bushes, long grass, and the local willow scrub. The ball was eight to nine inches down deep in the stuff. I saw the stroke and watched the ball fly dead straight onto the green, almost one-hundred-fifty yards away, into an almost head on wind. I don't know how one measures golfing strength, but Arnold Palmer is certainly a golfing giant.
—HENRY COTTON, ON ARNOLD PALMER'S THIRD-ROUND SHOT ON THE 16TH HOLE AT THE 1961 OPEN

• • •

Nobody can be satisfied until he wins the British Open Championship.
—ARNOLD PALMER, AFTER WINNING THE 1961 OPEN CHAMPIONSHIP AT ROYAL BRIKDALE

• • •

When Palmer went [in the early 1960s] all the other Americans went, too, and the British Open was restored to its former majesty.
—FORMER USGA EXECUTIVE DIRECTOR FRANK HANNIGAN

• • •

Another authentic American hero was born out of the gloom and crusty old atmosphere of golf on the linksland of Britain. In a playoff for the British Open . . . , young Tom Watson finally became a Champion, a new person, and one hellacious player.
—DAN JENKINS, IN *SPORTS ILLUSTRATED*, AFTER WATSON WON THE 1975 OPEN

• • •

When Ballesteros triumphed at the British Open in 1979, for his first major win, he hit so few fairways off the tee that he was often mistaken for a gallery marshall.
—DAN JENKINS

• • •

This was one of those rare occasions when golf managed to get the dramatic balance right, leaving the stars to play their allotted roles and confining the light relief to the supporting players.
—PETER DOBEREINER ON THE 1993 OPEN, WON BY GREG NORMAN

• • •

The greatest links player of all time deserves to play the Open as long as he wants, in my opinion. If I don't win, I'll certainly be rooting for Tom Watson.
—JUSTIN ROSE, BEFORE THE 2009 OPEN

• • •

Even the Taliban are rooting for you.
—THOMAS FRIEDMAN, IN AN E-MAIL SENT TO TOM WATSON FROM AFGHANISTAN DURING THE 2009 OPEN

• • •

Golf is such a strong thread running through the lives of so many Scots, even those who don't play. Everyone at least knows someone who does play, so they understand the passion in the game. Of course, I think my winning five Open championships helps, too.
—TOM WATSON, ON THE WARM RECEPTION HE RECEIVES FROM THE OPEN GALLERY

• • •

Tom Watson

CREDIT: Ian Tilbrook

Hey, I won my championship. I don't know what those other two guys were playing.
—Hubert Green, after finishing third, 11 strokes behind Jack Nicklaus and Tom Watson in the 1977 *Duel in the Sun*

• • •

Just goes to show what a demanding test of golf this is.
—Lee Westwood, after Tiger Woods missed the cut at the 2009 Open

• • •

I hadn't been at all sure that I would be standing up there beside that trophy—a high ball hitter like me who couldn't handle hard linksland fairways.
—Jack Nicklaus, after winning the 1966 Open

• • •

I honestly believe this is only the beginning. I think I can play great golf until I'm forty-five.
—Greg Norman, after shooting a final round 64 during the 1989 Open Championship, and losing by one stroke

• • •

I didn't go over to the British Open set on wrestling the Claret Jug out of anyone's hands and bringing it back to Duluth, Georgia . . . . I love links golf. . . . You have to hit all the shots. You can't hide anything.
—Stewart Cink, the 2009 Open champion

• • •

The greens are firm. The fairways are firm. When you add the wind to it, the ball doesn't stop right by the hole. You have to filter it in there.
—Tom Watson

• • •

Gene Sarazan   CREDIT: Arambat

The PGA Championship

To survive a week of match play such as this, one has to be able to play a super brand at all times.
—*PROFESSIONAL GOLFER OF AMERICA* (1923), ON THE MATCH-PLAY FORMAT OF THE PGA IN ITS EARLY YEARS

• • •

I wouldn't have entered the PGA, the way I was playing, had I not been defending champion.
—GENE SARAZAN, AFTER WINNING THE 1923 PGA

• • •

I wonder which one of you fellows will be second this year.
—WALTER HAGEN TO OTHER GOLFERS BEFORE THE START OF THE 1925 PGA, WHICH HE WON

• • •

I didn't win it. They tossed it to me. What's a guy going to do? A lot of them had me on the ropes.
—WALTER HAGEN, AFTER WINNING HIS FOURTH STRAIGHT PGA IN 1927

• • •

I can't remember. I might have left it in a cab.
—WALTER HAGEN, AFTER LOSING THE PGA IN 1928, WHEN ASKED BY PGA OFFICIALS ABOUT THE LOCATION OF THE WANNAMAKER CUP.

• • •

Though I won the PGA in 1949 and 1951, that first win in 1942 was the biggest, and one I enjoyed the most. It happened just so quick.
—SAM SNEAD

• • •

CREDIT: Thomas Northcutt

The PGA is as tough a test of golf as there is. Try playing 36 holes every day for a week and see how you feel on the seventh day.
—Byron Nelson, 1945

• • •

You probably think I'm happy over winning this tournament, but I'm not. I hate to beat these men. They have to go back to their clubs and tell how they were beaten. The physical ordeal of the PGA takes too much out of a man. I just don't want to put myself through that anymore.
—Ben Hogan, after playing his last PGA Championship in 1948

• • •

No other championship in golf calls for so much combined physical stamina, nerve control, courage, and skill.
—Horton Smith

• • •

This tournament is an endurance contest. You've got to be strong
to get through it.
—CARY MIDDLECOFF

• • •

We either had to go forward and make it a championship that
will rival the U.S. Open, or we play it every year at Dunedin as a
member's tournament.
—A PGA OFFICIAL ON THE DECISION TO MAKE THE PGA AN
OPEN TOURNAMENT

• • •

I don't think a tournament with such a long history and tradition
of its own wants to be thought of as "U.S. Open: The Sequel."
—PETER JACOBSEN

• • •

CREDIT: iStockphoto/Thinkstock

The best player didn't win today—but I'm glad I did.
—1961 PGA Champion Jerry Barber

• • •

Having won nine majors, I am extremely proud that two of these
came in the PGA Championship.
—Gary Player

• • •

It was an honor to be an eyewitness to history being made. It is
bordering on the unbelievable that he has won so many major
events and is still so young, and did it with such ease.
—Bruce Crampton, after four-time PGA winner Jack
Nicklaus's 1973 victory

• • •

I'd love to say, "Hey, I won the PGA."
—Arnold Palmer, who never won a PGA

• • •

One of my attributes is that when I get ahead, I seldom fold. The trouble is I don't get in the lead often enough.
—Dave Stockton, after winning the 1976 PGA Championship

• • •

Were you in prison in 1984? Maybe you didn't get copies of the newspaper there?
—1984 PGA winner Lee Trevino, after being told by a reporter in 1986 that he hadn't won a major in a long time

• • •

Norman stood on the fringe and looked on incredulously. The two words he uttered were the same two that are heard on flight recorders retrieved from plane wreckage. The printable version is "oh, no."
—LARRY DORMAN, ON THE 1986 PGA

• • •

Where can you go to have a good cry?
— MIKE REID, AFTER LOSING A THREE-STROKE LEAD ON THE LAST THREE HOLES OF THE 1989 PGA

• • •

Turns out the three guys ahead of me on the alternates list [for the 1991 PGA] had pulled out . . . .
And then Nick Price withdrew because his wife was about to give birth to their first child. So thanks to Sue Price, I made it into the 1991 PGA Championship!
—JOHN DALY, FROM *MY LIFE IN AND OUT OF THE ROUGH*

• • •

I can't club this guy. He hits it longer than anybody I've ever seen.
—JEFF MEDLEN, JOHN DALY'S CADDIE AT THE 1991 PGA

• • •

Kill it, John, just kill it.
—ADVICE GIVEN TO JOHN DALY BY HIS CADDIE, JEFF
MEDLEN, AS DALY PREPARED TO HIT TEE SHOTS AT THE 1991
PGA

• • •

Winning the [1995] British Open was sweet but not as rowdy
and cool as [winning the 1991 PGA]. It was cool going through
the crowd high-fiving everybody. My right hand was so sore after
that week.
—JOHN DALY

• • •

The PGA is the break-through major that either confirms the
greatness of a player or spins the golf world on a crazy tangent.
—CAMERON MORFIT, GOLF MAGAZINE

• • •

John Daly

CREDIT: mandj98

It feels like a finally got a monkey off my back—a whole troupe of them.
—Nick Price, after winning the 1992 PGA, his first major

• • •

The crowd was mumbling about Nicklaus, but I didn't need them to tell me the Bear was coming.
—Hal Sutton, who won the PGA in 1993

• • •

All you have to say is Tiger at Valhalla, Daly at Crooked Stick, Micheel at Oak Hill and today's golf fans know what you mean because they saw it.
—Jim Nantz

• • •

You never know in life, this might be my last win as a golfer. But this is a great day.
—Y.E. Yang, after he defeated Tiger Woods at the 2009 PGA to become the first Korean man to win a major championship

• • •

To be honest, I wanted to go out there and prove people wrong. That's what I did. It took me all of four weeks to get my game back in shape and get out of my mini-slump, and this is the result.
—Rory McIlroy, after winning the 2012 PGA Championship

• • •

One could argue that during this decade the PGA Championship has become the most exciting of the four majors.
—Clifton Brown, 2003

• • •

CREDIT: Ingram Publishing/Thinkstock

PART FIVE

Miscellany

Thoughts on politicians, pressure, prayer and more.

It is one of the irrefutable truths of golf that your game is significantly hampered by standing too near the ball . . . . This is especially true after you have hit it.
—ANONYMOUS

• • •

Golf is a good walk spoiled.
—MARK TWAIN

• • •

Mark Twain said golf is a good walk spoiled—from which we can only conclude he'd either had a bad day on the course or, more likely, never played at all. A walk is a missed opportunity for golf.
—ANDREW GREIG

• • •

Golf is a game where you yell 'fore,' shoot six, and write five.
—PAUL HARVEY

• • •

Golf is good for the soul. You get so mad at yourself you forget to hate your enemies.
—WILL ROGERS

• • •

How can a game have such an effect on a man's soul?
—DAVID L. COOK

• • •

Very lately I have come to a sort of Presbyterian attitude toward tournament golf. I can't get away from the idea of predestination.
—BOBBY JONES, FROM DOWN THE FAIRWAY

• • •

I'm not a good enough golfer to play golf every day.
—DREW BLEDSOE

• • •

The uglier a man's legs are, the better he plays golf. It's almost a law.
—H.G. Wells

• • •

Golf? Golf's not a sport.
—Mike Krzyzewski

• • •

Golf is a day spent in a round of strenuous idleness.
—William Wordsworth

• • •

I like golf because when somebody tells the gallery to be quiet, they get quiet. Try that in baseball and they get louder.
—Mark McGwire

• • •

CREDIT: iStockphoto/Thinkstock

It took me seventeen years to get 3,000 hits in baseball. I did it in one afternoon on the golf course.
—Hank Aaron

• • •

I like golf because I can go out and hit a little white ball that doesn't move and doesn't hit back. It should be easy, but it isn't.
—Lawrence Taylor

• • •

My best score is 103. But I've only been playing fifteen years.
—Alex Karras

• • •

I just can't find it when I hit it.
—Jerry West

• • •

Golf is a fickle game, and must be wooed to be won.
—WILLIE PARK JNR

• • •

No other sport asks participants to call penalties on themselves
or to play their own foul balls.
—GEORGE FULLER, FROM *I GOLF, THEREFORE I AM—NUTS*

• • •

They call it 'golf' because all the other four-letter words were
taken.
—RAYMOND FLOYD

• • •

If there is a ball on the green and one in the bunker, mine's in the
bunker.
—VANCE NEUDORF

• • •

CREDIT: iStockphoto/Thinkstock

CREDIT: Jupiterimages

My dear young lady, I'm not losing my temper. I'm merely trying
to play some golf.
—CARY GRANT AS DAVID HUXLEY IN *BRINGING UP BABY*

● ● ●

Golfing excellence goes hand in hand with alcohol, as many an
Open and Amateur champion has shown.
—HENRY LONGHURST

● ● ●

Whiff - "Familiar term widely misused to describe particularly
fast and powerful style of practice swing intentionally made
directly over the ball."
—HENRY BEARD, FROM *GOLFING: A DUFFER'S DICTIONARY*

● ● ●

You can talk to a fade, but a hook won't listen.
—Lee Trevino

• • •

A curious thing I have noticed about golf is that a festering griev-
ance sometimes does wonders for a man's drive. It's as if pent-up
emotion added zip to his swing.
—P.G. Wodehouse

• • •

The greatest thing about golf, there's no end to it unless you're
dead. You just go from here to the Senior Tour.
—Fuzzy Zoeller

• • •

A man who could retain through his golfing career the almost scornful confidence of the non-player would be unbeatable.
—P.G. WODEHOUSE, FROM *GOLF WITHOUT TEARS*

• • •

It was at Winged Foot where member David Mulligan couldn't start a round without getting a ball on the fairway, often hit a second shot, and the word "Mulligan" entered the golfing lexicon in 1937.
—ART SPANDER, *OAKLAND TRIBUNE*

• • •

It's the putter. I don't know whether it's a physical thing or mental. A neurological thing, perhaps. The brain tells the body one thing, but the body doesn't listen. Nerves. Yips.
—NICK PRICE, ON WHICH CLUB IS THE FIRST TO SUCCUMB TO A GOLFER'S AGE

• • •

I'm just a grown caddie still studying golf.
—HARVEY PENICK

• • •

It's the Indian and not the arrow.
—FUZZY ZOELLER, ON THE INCREASING POPULARITY OF THE
LONG PUTTER

• • •

Maybe it's because I'm in the rough so much that I get to know
them all personally.
—ARNOLD PALMER, WHEN ASKED WHY HIS FANS WERE SO
DEVOTED TO HIM

• • •

Not even God can hit a 1-iron.
—LEE TREVINO

• • •

God intended this to be a golf course.
—Architect Donald Ross, when surveying the property that would become Oakland Hills

• • •

That does look like good exercise. But what is the little white ball for?
—Ulysses S. Grant

• • •

I'll be damned if I give up my game of golf.
—President William Howard Taft, when he refused to meet with the president of Chile

• • •

It would seem incredible that anyone would care one way or the other about your playing golf, but I have received hundreds of letters from the West protesting it. I myself play tennis, but that game is a little more familiar; besides, you never saw a photograph of me playing tennis, I am careful about that; photographs of me on horseback, yes; tennis, no. And golf is fatal.
—Theodore Roosevelt, in a letter to William Howard Taft

• • •

President Eisenhower has given up golf for painting. It takes fewer strokes.
—Bob Hope

• • •

Whenever I play with him [President Gerald Ford], I usually try to make it a foursome—the President, myself, a paramedic, and a faith healer.
—Bob Hope

• • •

President Gerald Ford

President John F. Kennedy and friends play golf

Show me a man who plays a good game of golf and I'll show you a man who is neglecting something.
—JOHN F. KENNEDY

• • •

He could hit it a ton . . . but often had no idea where it was going.
—BEN BRADLEE, ON JOHN F. KENNEDY'S GOLF GAME

• • •

His setup position is too round-shouldered and stiff-legged, as though he were staring down a copy of his next State of the Union address.
—A GOLF DIGEST ASSESSMENT OF RICHARD M. NIXON'S GOLF SWING (1970)

• • •

He doesn't know he can't hit the ball through the trunk of a tree.
—JACK NICKLAUS ON GERALD R. FORD

• • •

One lesson you'd better learn if you want to be in politics is that you never go out on a golf course and beat the president.
—LYNDON JOHNSON

• • •

It's amazing how many people beat you at golf when you're no longer president.
—GEORGE H.W. BUSH

• • •

I call upon all nations to do everything they can to stop these terrorist killers. Thank you. Now watch this drive.
—GEORGE W. BUSH (2002)

• • •

I don't want some mom whose son may have recently died to see the commander in chief playing golf.
—George W. Bush, on his decision to stop playing golf in 2003

• • •

Golf is like life in a lot of ways . . . All the biggest wounds are self-inflicted.
—Bill Clinton

• • •

I don't know whether he shot an 83 or 283 or 483. You'll never really know.
—Bob Dole, in 1996, on the accuracy of Bill Clinton's golf scores

• • •

Hey, guys, that was pretty good, right? That almost made up for my 20-yard drive.
—BARACK OBAMA IN 2008

• • •

Since the 1980 presidential election, a curious trend has emerged: Jimmy Carter. Walter Mondale. Michael Dukakis. Bob Dole. Al Gore. John Kerry. John McCain. None of them played golf. All of them tasted bitter defeat. All of them lost to golfers.
—DON VAN NATTA, JR., *ESPN THE MAGAZINE*

• • •

I can say with great confidence that they will not wrap up the 18th hole and come out and say that we have a deal.
—WHITE HOUSE PRESS SECRETARY JAY CARNEY, BEFORE PRESIDENT OBAMA'S ROUND OF GOLF WITH JOHN BOEHNER IN 2011

• • •

President Barack Obama and Vice President Joe Biden practice putting on the south lawn of the White House

CREDIT: Pete Souza/
The White House

One time when I was president I . . . was playing a course in Calgary, and after I made a 30-foot birdie putt on 16 I had a chance to shoot 78 or 79 even if I bogeyed out. But I had to quit because I was late to give a speech.
—BILL CLINTON

• • •

Nobody wants to hear about anyone else's round [of golf].
—DAN JENKINS

• • •

No pretty woman can miss a single shot without a man giving her some poor advice.
—HARVEY PENICK, FROM HIS *LITTLE RED BOOK*

• • •

Through time all other griefs may cure,
All other hurts may mend,
The miseries of golf endure:
To them there is no end.
—EDGAR A. GUEST, FROM "COMFORTLESS"

• • •

Golf is a puzzle without an answer.
—GARY PLAYER

• • •

The place of the father in the modern family is a very small one,
especially if he plays golf.
—BERTRAND RUSSELL

• • •

Although golf was originally restricted to the wealthy, over-weight Protestants, today it's open to anyone who owns hideous clothing.
—DAVE BARRY

• • •

The talking golfer is the most pronounced pest of our complex modern civilization, and the most difficult to deal with.
—P.G. WODEHOUSE, FROM *GOLF WITHOUT TEARS*

• • •

I never really felt nerves swimming. Jumping in the pool is what I've done for 20 years. But I get nervous playing golf in front of strangers. I hate it. "Fore!" is something you hear from me a lot.
—MICHAEL PHELPS

• • •

My friend . . . has a great description of me teeing off: He says I look like I'm between two subway cars with a foot on each platform.
—MICHAEL J. FOX

• • •

Playing God is the easiest of all. . . . Golf is hard. Very, very hard.
—MORGAN FREEMAN

• • •

Retire to what? I already play golf and fish for a living.
—JULIUS BOROS

• • •

Rich guys with fast backswings.
—TOMMY ARMOUR, WHEN ASKED WHOM HE LIKED PLAYING AGAINST IN RETIREMENT

• • •

CREDIT: minds-eye

The golf is good, the toupees are awful. I may be bald, but I'll never glue one of those divots on my head, and that's a promise.
—Tom Weiskopf, on the Senior Tour

● ● ●

Sometimes you just like to stand there in the middle of the green and scream as loud as you can. But we're perfect gentlemen.
—Raymond Floyd

● ● ●

Many men are more faithful to their golf partners than to their wives, and have stuck with them longer.
—John Updike, from *The Camaraderie of Golf II*

● ● ●

Why does my wife—and by extension, virtually everyone else's
wife—hate golf?
—David Owen, from *Grown Men on Spring Break*

● ● ●

Give me golf clubs, fresh air and a beautiful partner, and you can
keep the clubs and fresh air.
—Jack Benny

● ● ●

You know the old rule: he who have the fastest cart never have to
play a bad lie.
—Mickey Mantle

● ● ●

A caddie is someone who accompanies a golfer and didn't see the
ball either.
—Anonymous

● ● ●

The most common problems associated with being a caddie [in eighteenth-century Scotland] were the lack of regular employment and the temptation of alcohol.
—KEVIN MCGIMPSEY, FROM *GOLF: IMPLEMENTS AND MEMORABILIA*

• • •

There's really nothing you can do for your man . . . . You can give him good yardages, tell him how you see the knobs of the greens, is it uphill, is it downhill, all that. You can throw grass clippings in the air until the sky falls down, tell him the direction of the breeze and how hard it's blowing . . . .You can put the club in his and, tell him to hit the soft six or the hard seven. But you cannot take the bloody swing for him.
—IAN BOTTOMLEY, PROFESSIONAL CADDIE

• • •

I never kick my ball in the rough or improve my lie in a sand trap. For that I have a caddy.
—BOB HOPE

• • •

Bob Hope's swing? I've seen better swings on a condemned playground.
—BING CROSBY

• • •

It is no big secret that the game of golf requires grave concentration to be played decently, so let me say right off that it is not altogether to your advantage while you're standing over a 5-iron shot to be thinking: "I've got to remember to get some Freon in the Toyota."
—DAN JENKINS, FROM "MY SEMI-TOUGH RETURN TO PLAYING GOLF"

• • •

A Golf-Dependent Personality can cheerfully whistle while screwing new spikes into his golf shoes the morning after playing two rounds of dreary, life-threatening golf.
—DAVID OWEN, FROM *GROWN MEN ON SPRING BREAK*

• • •

Miscellany

CREDIT: iStockphoto/Thinkstock

The correlation between thinking well and making successful shots is not 100 percent. But the correlation between thinking badly and unsuccessful shots is much higher.
—BOB ROTELLA, FROM *GOLF IS NOT A GAME OF PERFECT*

• • •

Choking is a stage of the yips. Both of them have to do with being unable to study, to concentrate. It's true that a golfer can get a nerve problem that can't be helped. Those are the yips.
—ARNOLD PALMER

• • •

I broke down completely . . . The yips took me then and tore me apart. The rest of my game was never better but on the carpet I was a zombie. Over the ball, I felt like someone else's hands held the putter. All control was gone.
—SAM SNEAD, FROM *THE EDUCATION OF A GOLFER*

• • •

It was what ultimately drove the pros out of the game to the teaching jobs at the country clubs, setting the balls on tees for the girls in the Pucci pants who came down for their two free gift lessons of the summer.
—GEORGE PLIMPTON, ON THE YIPS

• • •

Nothing. Once you've had them you've got them.
—TOMMY ARMOUR, WHEN ASKED BY ANOTHER GOLFER HOW HE RID HIMSELF OF THE YIPS

• • •

One thing elevates golf from the realm of games to the world of sports. The choke factor . . . .Basically, golf offers us the spectacle of people under enormous strain unraveling before our, and their own, disbelieving eyes.
—THOMAS BOSWELL, FROM *THE CHOKE FACTOR*

• • •

I used to think pressure was standing over a four-foot putt knowing I had to make it. I learned that real pressure was 65 people waiting for their food with only 30 minutes left on their lunch-hour break.
—AMY ALCOTT ON WAITRESSING IN THE OFFSEASON

• • •

It's a good bet that in almost every golf club there's at least one member who hits the ball as it should be hit, has a sound style, is keen, practices a lot, yet who never seems to make the grade . . . . The reason is that he has mastered all the departments of the game but the most vital one—his nerves.
—NORMAN VON NIDA, FROM *GOLF IS MY GAME* (1957)

• • •

We all choke. You just try to choke last.
—TOM WATSON

• • •

Too much cannot be said about tension and the need to avoid it. It probably ruins more golf shots than any other cause.
—Bobby Locke, from *On Golf* (1953)

• • •

Fear of any kind is the number one enemy of all golfers, regardless of ball-striking and shot-making capabilities. [Fear] happened to me before my early success enabled me to control my fear.
—Jack Nicklaus

• • •

Pro golfers putt more accurately from all distances when putting for par than when putting for birdie because they fear the bogie more than they desire the birdie.
—David Brooks

• • •

CREDIT: iStockphoto/Thinkstock

People don't understand how wonderful that feeling is—to be absolutely scared to death that you are not going to be able to perform. And then you do. You pull the shots off—sometimes to your own amazement. It's an incredible feeling. That being scared, that's fun.
—TOM KITE

• • •

The first step in fearless golf is to consciously make a decision not to be afraid, or maybe at least to not be afraid of being afraid.
—DR. GIO VALIANTE, FROM *FEARLESS GOLF: CONQUERING THE MENTAL GAME*

• • •

When I learned how to breathe I learned how to win.
—TOM WATSON

• • •

There's not as much pressure on the golf tour. Walking to the first tee is in no way comparable to walking through the jungle in combat.
—LARRY NELSON, GOLF PRO AND VIETNAM VETERAN

• • •

You're just assuming that I'm drunk because I'm driving a golf cart at 3:30 in the morning.
—BILL MURRAY, AFTER SWEDISH POLICE STOPPED HIM FOR DRIVING A GOLF CART THROUGH STOCKHOLM IN 2007

• • •

One is for temperament, one is for concentration, one is for anxiety and I forget what the other is for. Memory, I think.
—PAYNE STEWART, WHEN ASKED ABOUT THE ACUPUNCTURE NEEDLES IMPLANTED IN HIS EAR

• • •

Miscellany

CREDIT: Bernard Gagnon

Hope and fear, hope and fear, that's how people play golf. Not me.
No, not me. I see happiness, I see happiness.
—MOE NORMAN

• • •

Golf has swallowed Japan whole. People will do almost anything,
and pay almost anything, if it has anything to do with golf.
—RICK REILLY, FROM *LOVE THAT GOLF* (1989)

• • •

It is scarcely ever useful to count the enemy's chickens before
they are hatched . . . .A secret disbelief in the enemy's play is very
useful for match play.
—EXCERPT FROM *THE ART OF GOLF* (1892)

• • •

We knew we had it won. On 17 and 18 we were buying ice cream bars for the fans.
—BILL MURRAY, AFTER HE AND D.A. POINTS WON THE 2011 PEBBLE BEACH PRO-AM

• • •

I'm sorry, Charles, I've run out of ideas. I feel for you. I really do.
—TOM WATSON TO CHARLES BARKLEY, WITH WHOM HE WAS PAIRED AT A PRO-AM EVENT IN 2000

• • •

Low-handicap players don't like to let high-handicap players play through because they are not good enough and should know their station in life. By the same token, high handicappers don't like to let low-handicappers through because if low handicappers spent more time tending to their businesses they wouldn't be that good in the first place.
—PETER ANDREWS, FROM *THE SOCIAL ASPECT OF PLAYING THROUGH*

• • •

There are a lot of discriminatory golf courses out there, not just against blacks. The fight is on every level of discrimination, to make this game what it should be—enjoyable. All the rest is baggage that should be left at the clubhouse door.
—DEBORAH ANDERSON, FORMER PRESIDENT OF THE WOMEN'S SPORTS FOUNDATION

• • •

The idea that golf is mostly a rich old guy's sport is an exaggeration created by advertisers to appeal to the aspirational shopper.
—DAVID BROOKS

• • •

There we go! Miles and miles and miles!
—ASTRONAUT ALAN SHEPARD, AFTER HITTING A GOLF SHOT ON THE MOON

• • •

Alan Shepard didn't take a baseball or soccer ball to the moon. He took a 6 iron. Some folks will do anything to get a little extra distance on a drive!
—George Fuller, from *I Golf, Therefore I Am—Nuts*

• • •

Warmest congratulations to all of you on your great achievement and safe return. Please refer to Rules of Golf section on etiquette, paragraph 6, "Before leaving a bunker a player should carefully fill up all holes made by him therein."
—Telegram received by Alan Shepard , who played two shots of golf on the surface of the moon

• • •

There is a golf ball on the moon, left behind by Alan Shepard. But I hear the course isn't very well maintained.
—David Lindsay, from *Lost Balls, Great Holes*

• • •

One time I was complaining that my shot was going to wind up in the water. So my friend . . . told me that I should think positive. I told him okay, I was positive my shot was going to wind up in the water.
—YOGI BERRA

• • •

I can laugh at myself in some ways, but not when it comes to hitting bad shots. What's so funny about a shank?
—TOM WEISKOPF

• • •

Works and Authors Quoted

Books
Peter Alliss
  Alliss's 19th Hole: Trivial Delights from the World of Golf (2007)
  Golf: The Cure for a Grumpy Old Man (2009)
  Golf Heroes (2010)

David Barrett
  Making the Masters: Bobby Jones and the Birth of America's Greatest Golf Tournament (2012)
  Miracle at Merion: The Inspiring Story of Ben Hogan's Amazing Comeback and Victory at the 1950 U.S. Open (2010)

Henry Beard
   *Golf: An Unofficial and Unauthorized History of the World's
   Most Preposterous Sport* (2009)
   Golfing: A Duffer's Dictionary (2001)
   Mulligan's Laws (1993)

Tripp Bowden
   *Freddie & Me: Life Lessons from Freddie Bennett, Augusta
   National's Legendary Caddy Master* (2009)

Phil Callaway
   With God on the Golf Course (2002)

Malcolm Campbell
   The Scottish Golf Book (1999)

John Campaniotte and Catherine Lewis
   The PGA Championship: The Season's Final Major (2004)

Bill Chastain
   *Payne at Pinehurst: A Memorable U.S. Open in the Sandhills of
   Carolina* (2005)

Bob Charles
   Left-Handed Golf (1965)

Dale Concannon
   Golf: The Early Days (1995)

Works and Authors Quoted

David L. Cook
Seven Days in Utopia: Golf's Sacred Journey (2011)

Alistair Cooke
Golf: The Marvelous Mania (2007)

John Daly
My Life in and out of the Rough (2007)

James Dodson
American Triumvirate: Sam Snead, Byron Nelson, Ben Hogan, and the Modern Age of Golf (2012)

Myles Dungan
A Good Walk Spoiled: A Book of Golf Quotes (1994)

John Feinstein
A Good Walk Spoiled: Days and Nights on the PGA Tour (1995)
One on One: Behind the Scenes with the Greats in the Game (2012)

Steve Friedman
The Agony of Victory: When Winning Isn't Enough (2007)

George Fuller
I Golf, Therefore I Am—Nuts (2008)

W. Timothy Gallwey
The Inner Game of Golf (2009)

William Hallberg
  Perfect Lies: A Century of Great Golf Stories (1998)

Harold Horsfall Hilton
  Modern Golf (1913)

Ben Hogan
  Five Lessons: The Modern Fundamentals of Golf (1957)
  Power Golf (1948)

Jim Huber
  Four Days in July: Tom Watson, the 2009 Open Championship, and a Tournament for the Ages (2009)

Horace G. Hutchinson
  Golf: A Complete History of the Game (1905)

John R. Jenchura
  Golf—A Good Walk & Then Some: A Quintessential History of the Game (2010)

Dan Jenkins
  Fairways and Greens: The Best Golf Writing of Dan Jenkins (1994)
  Jenkins at the Majors (2010)

Tom Kite and Don Wade
  One Week in June: The U.S. Open (2010)

Rex Lardner
  Out of the Bunker and into the Trees (1960)

Works and Authors Quoted

Chris Lewis
The Scorecard Always Lies: A Year Behind the Scenes on the PGA Tour (2010)

Charles Lindsay
Lost Balls: Great Holes, Tough Shots, and Bad Lies (2005)

Bobby Locke
On Golf (1954)

Steve Lynas
The Complete Book of Golf: An Unrivalled Collection of Writing and Photography on the World's Fastest Growing Sport (2000)

Kevin McGimpsey
Golf: Implements and Memorabilia (1999)

Phil Mickelson
Secrets of the Short Game (2009)

Byron Nelson
How I Played the Game: An Autobiography (2006)

Jack Nicklaus
Golf My Way (1974)
My Most Memorable Shots in the Majors (1988)
Jack Nicklaus: My Story (2007)

Joseph Parent
The Zen of Golf: Mastering the Mental Game (2002)

Harvey Penick
   Harvey Pencik's Little Red Book (1991)

Gary Player
   Don't Choke: A Champion's Guide to Winning Under Pressure (2010)

Nick Price
   The Swing: Mastering the Principles of the Game (1999)

Bob Rotella
   Golf is Not a Game of Perfect (1995)

Lorne Rubenstein
   Moe and Me: Encounters with Moe Norman, Golf's Mysterious Genius (2012)

Mark Shaw
   Jack Nicklaus: Golf's Greatest Champion (2002)

Fred Shoemaker
   Extraordinary Golf: The Art of the Possible (1997)

Matthew Silverman
   Golf Miscellany: Everything You Always Wanted to Know about Golf (2012)

Sam Snead
   The Education of a Golfer (1962)

The Game I Love: Wisdom, Insight and Instruction from Golf's Greatest Player (1997)

Robert Sommers
The U.S. Open: Golf's Ultimate Challenge (1996)

John Stobbs
At Random Through the Green: A Collection of Writings about Golf (1966)

Lee Trevino
They Call Me Super Mex (1982)

John Updike
"Golf," The New York Times (1973)
Golf Dreams: Writings on Golf (1996)

Gio Valiante
Fearless Golf: Conquering the Mental Game (2005)

Ken Venturi
Getting Up and Down in One: My Fifty Years in Golf (2006)

Don Wade
"And then Justin told Sergio" . . . A Collection of the Greatest True Golf Stories Ever Told (2003)
"And Then Ch-Chi Told Fuzzy . . . " (1994)
"And then Tiger told the Shark . . . " (1999)
"And Then the Shark Told Justin . . . " (2000)

Talking on Tour (2003)
Herbert Warren Wind, Following Through (1985)

P.G. Wodehouse
Golf Without Tears (1999)
The Golf Omnibus (1996)
Fore!: The Best of Wodehouse on Golf (2008)

Tiger Woods
Golf My Way (2001)

Allan Zullo and Chris Rodell
Golf is a Funny Game (2008)

Periodicals
Golf Digest
Golfdigest.com
Golf Magazine
The Los Angeles Times
The New York Times
Oakland Tribune
Sports Illustrated

Index

Index